EVERYDAY
SPIRITUALITY
FOR EVERYONE

COVER PHOTO BY STEVE ZOLNO
(Enhanced by Terry Cullinane)
THE TEMPLE MOUNT, JERUSALEM:
Al-Aqsa Mosque and the Western Wall of the Jewish
Temple destroyed by the Romans in 70 AD. This is holy
ground for Jews, Christians, and Muslims.

EVERYDAY SPIRITUALITY FOR EVERYONE

by Steve Zolno

REGENT PRESS
Berkeley, California

paperback:
ISBN 13: 978-1-58790-562-9
ISBN 10: 1-58790-562-0

e-book:
ISBN 13: 978-1-58790-563-6
ISBN: 10: 1-58790-563-9

Library of Congress Cataloging-in-Publication Data

Names: Zolno, Steve, author.
Title: Everyday spirituality for everyone / by Steve Zolno.
Description: Berkeley, California : Regent Press, 2021. | Summary:
Identifiers: LCCN 2021007152 (print) | LCCN 2021007153 (ebook)
| ISBN 9781587905629 (paperback) | ISBN 1587905620 (paper-
back) | ISBN 1587905639 (ebook) | ISBN 9781587905636 (ebook)
Subjects: LCSH: Spirituality. | Religions. | Peace of mind.
Classification: LCC BL624 .Z65 2021 (print) | LCC BL624 (ebook)
| DDC x204--dc23
LC record available at https://lccn.loc.gov/2021007152
LC ebook record available at https://lccn.loc.gov/2021007153

Manufactured in the U.S.A.
Regent Press
Berkeley, California
www.regentpress.net
regentpress@mindspring.com

CONTENTS

INTRODUCTION . . . 1

THE QUEST . . . 7

THE PATH . . . 21

Searching for Fulfillment in Religion . . . 22

Other Paths to Fulfillment . . . 35

What All Paths Have in Common . . . 45

Tilting at Windmills . . . 50

THE GOAL . . . 55

Some Areas into Which We Divide the World . . . 60

The Nature of Forgiveness . . . 82

The Nature of Freedom . . . 82

The Nature of Truth . . . 83

Spirituality and Democracy . . . 84

Spirituality and Anger . . . 85

Spirituality and Humor . . . 86

Spirituality and Leadership . . . 87

Spirituality and Death . . . 88

Our Choice . . . 89

Where I Come From . . . 93

Ten Spiritual Principles . . . 98

INTRODUCTION

You might consider yourself religious or to be someone with no interest in religion at all. You may think of yourself as a spiritual person or have an aversion to anything that could be considered not of this world.

But regardless of what you think about religion or spirituality, you still are very much a spiritual person. Everyone not only has a spiritual side, but spirituality pervades each of our lives on a regular basis.

If you ever have loved someone or felt a connection with anyone or anything, you have had a spiritual experience. If you believe that you have not ever experienced a connection with another person or the world around you — but would like to — it is a spiritual experience you seek.

Spirituality — as I will use it in these pages — is what connects us with what is outside of ourselves: others, the world, or an unseen force that some call God. Spirituality is what brings us fulfillment as we experience those connections. When we truly engage with our surroundings we open ourselves to something beyond us. We move past the shell we have created in which we believe we are separate from the world.

Spirituality is not the exclusive realm of religion. It is a feeling – or state of mind – that already is an essential part of who we are, and to which we can return as we learn to recognize its nature.

We are born with a sense of connection to others and all that surrounds us. At first we don't differentiate between ourselves and the world. With time we begin to think we are separate from our surroundings. This is the viewpoint we create in our minds that allows us to function as individual beings. Although not often aware of it, our connection with what is around us continues as we consume what we need for survival, breathe in, and expel what our body rejects.

The human condition is one of perpetually seeking fulfillment. There is a constant and continual hole we try to fill with what we believe is missing, whether it be a relationship, a career, a new possession, knowledge, or interaction with a force beyond us. Our lives seem to be lacking what we really want most of the time, but we only are vaguely aware of what that might be.

Because we chronically see our lives as unfulfilled, the question we perpetually ask is not if anything is missing, but what is missing. Our spiritual practice or religion provides limited answers, but we think that if we only have the right experience – spiritual or other – we will be fulfilled.

When we find our lives lacking it is because at some level we believe we miss the connections we once knew. Even if we think that our life is essentially material – based on obtaining possessions or winning at competition – we still desire the feeling that comes from the recognition of others.

We hope that as we indulge – or even overindulge – in what we believe will bring us happiness, we will at last be able to arrive at that place of inner peace we seek. But after we do what we think will provide long-term satisfaction we find it fails to bring us what we most want. We experience a diminished reward when we return to the same well. Thus the fulfillment we desire cannot be attained by anything we pursue or acquire.

In the following pages we explore a variety of religious and non-religious paths. Then we examine what we might do – if anything – to bring about the lasting state of inner peace we seek.

What I have written here reflects my current views, which are subject to revision as I continue the never-ending process of learning. This body will meet its demise, but the essential nature of truth – which we only glimpse while on this planet – never changes. As expressed in Isaiah 40:7:

Surely the people is grass. The grass withers, the flower fades; but the word of our God shall stand forever.

Please note that I have not included a list of references in this book because my intent is experiential, not academic. Those who want to expand their knowledge of areas covered easily can research them online. Also, references to much of the material are included in my previous books, *The Future of Democracy* and *Truth and Democracy.*

The hero is the archetypical forerunner of mankind. His fate is the pattern in accordance with which the masses of humanity must live, and always have lived, however haltingly and distantly; and however short of the ideal man they have fallen, the stages of the hero myth have become constituent elements in the personal development of every individual.

– Eric Neumann, The Origins and History of Consciousness

THE QUEST

As far back as we can see, there always has been the myth of the hero: that larger-than-life individual whose journey results in eternal fulfillment. We look to our heroes as models for how to live in perfect faith. They represent us in pursuit of our most significant personal and spiritual goals. From the mythical warriors of ancient Greece, to the founders of our major religions, to the medieval knights, to our modern screen idols, our heroes show us the path to overcoming evil and all obstacles to happiness forever after.

As part of the human condition we have basic physical needs that must be met. Beyond that we continually pursue long-term fulfillment. We seek certainty in an uncertain world.

Our quest can take many forms: searching for rewarding friendships or relationships, pursuing a gratifying career, vying for popularity, working toward financial security, chasing fame, or aligning with a force beyond us. We pursue knowledge and understanding to guide our journey. We look to the insights of others or divine guidance to help us find our way. Behind each of our quests is the same goal. We want respite from the burdens that life thrusts upon us; we hope to arrive at a place of peace and tranquility.

Our heroes – whether male or female – represent our ideal selves. They can be real or mythical: religious figures, politicians, sports icons, actors, musicians, historical legends, civil rights leaders, media personalities, fictional characters, and even relatives or friends. Through them we experience our own catharsis.

The goal of our heroes – and thus each of us – is overcoming all challenges and vanquishing all foes. Their quest brings them – and us – the success and recognition we seek. They evoke a sense of security and satisfaction in a life well-lived.

Our heroes pursue our personal fulfillment for us. Whether in religion, entertainment, sports, politics, finance, medicine, or myth, we idealize those we believe can conquer life's hurdles. We see them as exuding a confidence and competence that allows them to tread a path above and beyond the ordinary. Our aspirations seem nearer our grasp as we imagine being just like them. They seem always to triumph, and our lives are transformed along with theirs, at least for a while.

The stories of our heroes beckon us back to a time when, in a place deep within us, we believe we experienced an enduring sense of well-being.

We vaguely remember a time of peace and harmony. Our myths represent the perennial story of an ideal world that now seems lost and to which we long to return – perhaps an Eden or the innocence of childhood. They provide a chance to revisit a place that – in our minds – we believe we once dwelled.

Some writers have called the state we seek "the eternal return." We say to ourselves: "If only..." and then complete that thought with hope for a change in our circumstances – or the world – that we believe will bring our long-awaited happiness at last.

Our own lives seem mundane compared with those of our heroes. The exceptions are times when we experience a deep connection to others, immersion in activities that totally engage us, times of great insight, or episodes of spiritual inspiration. But recapturing those moments seems elusive.

The circumstances of our lives often bring disappointment. We pursue a goal of fulfillment that continually seems out of reach. We remain disillusioned as long-term satisfaction remains just beyond us. If we don't receive the nurturance we seek in personal interactions we blame the other person. Our work, though perhaps at times rewarding, fails to fill the emptiness we feel inside. Whether poor or rich, our possessions never are enough to bring us the happiness we seek. The religion or belief system that guides us is rewarding only for brief periods. And our other interests – such as food, drink, drugs, or recreational activities – bring only temporary satisfaction.

Fulfillment is something we hope to experience at some future time or place other than the here and now. Except for those rare moments when others or our world meet our hopes or expectations, our quest is never-ending. Behind our yearning for rewarding relationships is a wish to ignite a feeling of connection with another person; behind our hope for a satisfying career is a desire to be acknowledged as a valid human being; behind our craving to acquire more money or objects is a wish to be recognized as a worthy individual; behind our spiritual search is a desire to feel intimately engaged with a divine force.

But relationships, careers, possessions, spiritual practice and all else we pursue never in themselves are enough to satisfy us for long. Nothing we try seems to grant us long-term peace because our minds always return to emphasizing what is missing. It is a lost feeling of fulfillment we seek, but we don't know how to reignite it. Despite repeated disappointments, we cling to a hope that our next pursuit will help us reach our goal. But our ideas of what will bring ultimate satisfaction — in themselves — never can provide sustained fulfillment. Only a clear understanding of what we really want that goes beyond our ideas — and learning to gain direct access to that — can make us feel whole.

In our minds we believe we once experienced a state of connection between ourselves, others and the world. We were born to universal consciousness and then slowly learned to think of ourselves as separate individuals. It is to that original perspective we seek to return. We yearn for that place where the sense of "I" we now take for granted did not yet exist.

To function in the world, we assume an identity. It includes what we consider our gender, our race, our beliefs, our interests, and the groups to which we think of ourselves as belonging. It also includes the talents and abilities – as well as the limitations – we see in ourselves. Our education – first at home and then in a school setting – expands our idea of who we are as we work our way toward adulthood and hope to attain the skills we need to become competent members of society.

Suddenly, according to the standards of our culture, we supposedly arrive at the role of a fully-formed adult ready to navigate life. We strive to fulfill our obligation as a cog in the machinery of our society. But if we are honest with ourselves, we never really become totally competent to successfully steer our way in a complex world. Reality is vast and confusing. Our understanding – and the predictions we base on it – often falter. Unlike our heroes, our efforts fall short. In our careers, relationships, our spiritual and other pursuits, our mastery never is complete.

So we plod on with no certainty of success in

our quest except when we experience fulfillment through our heroes. They too struggle, but unlike us, overcome all obstacles. They pursue the ultimate good, although at times they may need to bend the rules in their quest for the triumph of what is just. When our heroes encounter uncertainty they draw on their infinite well of talent and inspiration. Their ship may veer off course, but we know eventually it will be righted. We may falter, but they represent the quest for doing what is right; for bringing courage and insight to every task.

Our heroes dwell in a world where good and evil are clear. Their actions rise above the ordinary as they pursue adventures that ennoble them, us and our planet. They take us on a journey in pursuit of the good even when they act badly in that pursuit. Unlike us, they never are disillusioned. They encounter each challenge with energy and resolve as they wend their way past every obstacle.

But there is a profound difference between the lives of our heroes and our own. In the world of our heroes, the journey has a clear destination that will restore them – and us – to peace and fulfillment. But in our real lives – both private and public – our struggle is ongoing. As long as we live, our story has no conclusion. The vision we hold of the good life and a just society – and our actions to achieve them – must continually be renewed.

The world around us is a vast assortment of sights and sounds that we once hoped we would learn to navigate. As we matured, our focus narrowed to specific short and long-term goals. But in the real world there never has been – and never can be – an end we can point to as that moment when we have fulfilled our ultimate vision. At that point life would lose its direction. But also – except in our minds – we never ultimately are defeated. If we are to move forward, our vision must continually be reimagined to fit the ever-changing reality around us.

We often are uncertain about which leaders to follow. There are those who claim that the welfare of all of humanity is intertwined, and others who only emphasize the benefits of individuals or some groups. There are those who champion human dignity, and those who denigrate it. We are told by some leaders that all people are deserving, and by others that some are not. It is easier to cling to one view for simplicity, without thinking through whether it leads to a united and functional, or divided and dysfunctional, world.

At any point in time we have a choice. We can continue to remain in the world of our myths where we hope our fantasies will be fulfilled.Or we can bring the idealism of a world that is just for all to our everyday interactions. Our inner world can emerge from the shadow of our minds to guide us rather than remaining just a place to escape from reality.

But doing this requires clarifying our most essential vision. We then need to apply that vision in our everyday lives. We all want to see ourselves as important players who can make a difference. Bringing the lessons of our myths and religions into our lives requires a willingness – and an ability – to make choices that reflect our values. So – as do our heroes – we need to commit ourselves to clarifying and enacting our direction. The clearer our vision, the more likely we will be able to move past disappointment and disillusionment in our quest for fulfillment.

But keeping our vision in mind as we ride along our bumpy path is a continual challenge. In the real world right and wrong – good and bad – are not as clear as in our myths. Identifying the threat and the enemy is not as easy. How do we move decisively toward implementing our vision? How do we clarify which actions – and people – stand in our way? What is required on our part to overcome them?

Situations and people continually disappoint us as we compare them with our idea of how they should be. But seeing this also may point to the possibility that our expectations get in our way. Encountering others and our world as we find them – rather than how we expect them to be – may allow us to interact with a more realistic version of reality. This then may increase our chance for satisfaction and success as we move forward in sync with how things — and people — really are.

Our judgments can obstruct our view and affect our actions. Good and evil often are the creation of our minds rather than attributes of reality. Good or bad acts – by others or ourselves – only are a part of who we are. They don't make a person good or bad. At our core we remain the same as when we are born. But in our minds we assign a positive or negative value to nearly every person and situation we encounter. As we see ourselves doing this we can begin to look beyond our judgments and move forward based on a more realistic view.

We can compare reality with our ideal as we retreat into disappointment, or we can open to the infinite nature of others, our world, and ourselves as we continually reshape our ideas. As we do this we look deeper into the essence of others as we expand our own internal depth of feeling and compassion.

We started life in a place of connection to the world and of deep feeling, then lost that sense of connection when we began to believe in ourselves as separate. We have sought a return to that sense of connection throughout our lives.

But the place we started can become our internal compass. We once knew very little but were open to whatever we encountered. We may once again learn to evoke that openness and bring it more fully into our lives and actions.

In a very real way we create ourselves as a person connected to the world around us who is able to overcome our challenges, or a person isolated and overwhelmed by forces beyond our control. Finding and nurturing that place within that feels connected to others and our surroundings leads us to depend less on circumstances as we move forward and shape our destiny. It allows us to bring a renewed clarity and commitment to our ongoing quest. How we view ourselves, others and our world – connected or separate – is a continual choice we make.

Even if we were to succeed at getting exactly what we think we want, or the world would comply with our every wish, that still would not provide long-term satisfaction. It is the full experience of our innermost feelings on an ongoing basis we seek, and only we – not others or the world – can grant that to us. Our real task never is accomplished once and forever. But as we are guided by our vision of connectedness to others and our world, our joy is in pursuing, not possessing, our ultimate goal.

We slowly can learn to bring our most essential self – that knows of its connections to the world – to the challenges of each moment. But even striving with all our might – and engaging all our resources – still doesn't bring us to long-term happiness. We carry our past within, including our joys and traumas, which largely obscures our perception of the present. The nature of truth, and its ability to guide us in our quest, remains elusive. So then, as we humbly acknowledge our human limitations, we open ourselves to guidance from a force beyond us.

Chronic remorse, as all the moralists are agreed, is a most undesirable sentiment. If you have behaved badly, repent, make what amends you can and address yourself to the task of behaving better next time. On no account brood over your wrongdoing. Rolling in the muck is not the best way of getting clean.

– Aldous Huxley, BRAVE NEW WORLD

THE PATH

Since the dawn of human consciousness, people have sought to understand the force that governs the universe and be guided by that knowledge. We have chosen countless routes on which to tread our spiritual and worldly paths: from the rituals of primitive societies, to the structures of our religions, to science, to the everyday pursuit of happiness.

Some of our paths appear to work — at least for a while — to bring us success in our quest, and others seem not to work at all. Among them are religious practice, human relationships, career advancement, financial pursuits, competition with others, civic engagement, self-improvement, the arts, food and drink, personality cults, body worship, meditation, exercise, sex, massage, yoga, various therapies, consciousness-altering drugs, and seeking truth, for just a partial list.

Birth itself is a shock to the human psyche. It separates us from a warm, nurturing environment as it thrusts us into the world. From then on we seek relief from that trauma by attempting to return to a sense of connection with what surrounds us.

Searching for Fulfillment in Religion

Many people remain committed to the traditional religion of their parents and ancestors, but new practices often are adopted by groups and individuals that they find compatible with their revised view of spiritual truth.

Most religions evolve over time, but some – like Christianity under the Reformation – have experienced violent upheavals. Modern reforms have included accepting women as leaders, admitting minorities into the flock, and allowing worship in contemporary languages.

Shamanic Ritual

Ancient tribes – and even some remote ones in our day – relied on shamans, or priests, to connect with the divine. Shamanic rituals explore the mysteries of the worlds seen and unseen. They intend to bring the participant into alignment with the supernatural force that dwells everywhere and provide success in areas such as the hunt, procuring rainfall, and defeating one's enemies.

Hinduism

Historians consider Hinduism – with its pantheon of gods and practices – the world's oldest major religion. Like many, it began as oral tradition with its origins lost in myth. Hindu gods represent every aspect of human understanding and aspiration. Brahman is the eternal universe itself. Brahma is the Creator of everything. The world periodically is destroyed by Shiva, which allows the cycle of death and rebirth of the universe to continue. Vishnu, the preserver, maintains the forms around us to which we have become attached.

Rama and Krishna are avatars – or appearances – of Vishnu. Rama is the ideal being who lives his life faithfully according to the laws of the universe, or Dharma, always aware of the consequences of his acts. His story is the subject of the epic *Ramayana*. Krishna is the god who knows all and teaches an appreciation of the infinite in our finite lives. He is best known for his appearance in the *Bhagavad Gita*, a part of the *Ramayana*, where he instructs his disciple, the warrior Arjuna, how to live fearlessly by bringing to mind the essence of the divine:

The Self, which dwells in the body of everyone, is eternal and never can be slain. (Bhagavad Gita 2–30)

The essence of Hindu belief is that for we who dwell on earth in our current incarnation, overcoming karma is the most important guiding principle. The word karma has become common in Western usage, even providing names for commercial ventures such as Good Karma Café. The principle of karma is the law of consequence, which means that the results of our actions eventually come back to us; we sow what we reap. But a more immediate effect of karma is that when we act in a way that is harmful we feel its effects in our alienation from others and a violation of our inner sense of right and wrong.

Buddhism

Buddhism is an outgrowth of Hinduism, just as Christianity is an outgrowth of Judaism. Although its origins are in India, it has spread throughout Southeast Asia and the world in various forms. The goal of Buddhism is inner peace through meditation and practice as taught by the Buddha, who is said to have achieved the perfect state of mind, or Nirvana, in the 5th century BCE. The story of the Buddha is that he was born rich, but perceived the suffering of others as he ventured into the world. He then sought to alleviate that suffering. Buddhism does not focus on deities, but on inner peace or "enlightenment." Its emphasis is on kindness, patience and compassion to align us with the Dharma. The *Metta Sutta* (1.8), attributed to The Buddha, tells us:

Radiate boundless love toward the entire world — above, below, and across — unhindered, without ill will, without enmity.

Egyptian Religions

The Egyptians had many gods. Some were idealized forms of animals that represented aspects of a godly personality, such as courage. The priests of the traditional religions held considerable power. The king who broke that tradition was Akhenaten, who in about 1350 BCE introduced the idea of the One God, or Aten, the sun god who shines on all without need for priestly intervention. Akhenaten built a new capital to honor his god, but upon his death, after a reign of seventeen years, Egypt returned to the old traditions; the priests regained their power and reestablished their multi-god religion. Some scholars believe that the story of the exit of the Israelites from Egypt at about that time actually is about those who refused to give up their belief in the One God. A quote from the Egyptian Book of the Dead, a guide for the afterlife, points to similarities between Egyptian beliefs and those of the Hebrews:

I am He who cannot be known.

Gods of the Greeks

The gods of the ancient Greeks were larger-than-life personalities who exemplified human yearning, including jealousy and lust for power. Statues of their gods were erected throughout the frequently warring city-states of the widespread Greek civilization that thrived for eight hundred years starting about 800 BCE. Many of their gods were adapted with new names by the Romans.

Zeus (Jupiter to the Romans), king of the gods, kept mortals and the other gods on edge by frequent fits of rage and jealousy. Hera (Juno) wife of Zeus, reaped revenge upon the objects of her husband's affection after his wild flings. Athena (Minerva), after whom the city of Athens was named, was the goddess of reason and wisdom. Aphrodite (Venus) was the goddess of love, sex, and beauty. Artemis (Diana) was the goddess of the hunt and protected the world of the living. Apollo, god of music and healing, guided the oracles at Delphi upon which the Greeks depended for guidance. Ares (Mars) was the god of war. Dionysus (Bacchus), son of Zeus, was the patron of indulgence, intoxication, and wild ritual. Hades ruled the underworld and Poseidon (Neptune) the sea.

But Greek philosophers also understood, and taught, about the One God underlying the rest. Antisthenes (445-360 BCE) wrote:

According to law, there are many gods; according to nature, only one.

The Greeks believed that we shape our lives

while on earth, after which our souls descend into the underworld governed by Hades. From there the good are sent to the Elysian Fields, and the worst to Tartarus. From the Elysian fields, one could try again for perfection by being reincarnated.

Canaanite Religions

Much information about the early religions mentioned in the Bible is lost in the shroud of pre-history. Carved images of gods have been found that were used by those who lived in Canaan (today's Israel and the area around it), many of which had human attributes. A statue of Ba'al, King of the gods, from about 1400 BCE, was discovered in the area of ancient Ugarit, a town in today's Syria that was abandoned in 1190 BCE. Its inhabitants believed in an underworld. Like the Hebrews they practiced animal sacrifice and considered some mountains to be holy. But little else is known of the religion from which Jewish tradition tells us that Abraham broke away to establish the origin of three major faiths that honor him – Judaism, Christianity and Muhammadism.

Judaism

As told in the Torah scrolls still used in Judaism that became the first five books of the Bible, Abram gave up the gods of his neighbors after hearing the voice of the One God. According to Genesis 17:5, Abram eventually became Abraham, or "a father of many nations," when he had his first child at age 99. As a young man, Abram dwelled in Haran, in "the land of Canaan," where he had a revelation that would form the basis of three major religions:

Now the Lord said to Abram, "Go from your country and your kindred and your father's house to the land that I will show you. And I will make of you a great nation, and I will bless you and make your name great, so that you will be a blessing. I will bless those who bless you, and he who dishonors you I will curse, and in you all the families of the earth shall be blessed." (Genesis 12:1-3)

Abram and his entourage left Canaan at a time of drought and dwelled in Egypt where he acquired considerable wealth, measured in cattle and precious metals. He then returned to Canaan. Eventually his descendent Joseph went again to Egypt and became a trusted advisor to the Pharaoh (Genesis 39), but in later generations that relationship deteriorated into slavery (Exodus 8).

The story of the slavery and exodus of the Israelites from Egypt is detailed in the Torah. Its origin is an oral tradition passed on for hundreds of years before it appeared in writing. Among the oldest Torah fragments found are priestly blessings similar to Exodus 20:6 ("...showing love to those who love me and keep my commandments...") excavated in Jerusalem at Ketef Hinnom, thought to be from about 600 BCE.

There is no historical evidence that the Jews were slaves in Egypt, but we do know that they eventually again came to dwell in Canaan. Despite tremendous challenges, the Jewish people have survived to this day. Whether it is their belief in One God, their legal system, or simply good luck, the Jewish religion still exists in multiple forms – Orthodox, Conservative, Reform, and many variants. The cornerstone of Judaism, the Shema, its most important daily prayer, begins:

Hear, O Israel: The Lord our God, The Lord is One. (Deuteronomy 6:4)

Christianity

Christianity started as a Jewish sect, also as an oral tradition, with its adherents expecting the imminent return of Jesus, whom they considered the Messiah. Eventually the next generation wrote down what is now the Christian Bible. The revelation of Jesus was forgiveness of all sins for those who accept him as their savior. Animal sacrifice was one of the most essential rituals of Judaism, but Christianity claimed that Jesus died as the ultimate sacrifice, making animal sacrifice no longer needed to absolve one's sins. Rather, the way to God is through his son:

I am the way and the truth and the life. No one comes to the Father except through Me. (JOHN 14:6)

Christianity has evolved into numerous branches and now is the world's largest religion.

Throughout much of its history there has been a division between those who teach that salvation is by works and those who believe it is by faith. The Catholic churches – both Eastern and Western – generally have held that the way to heaven is by good works. Reformers have claimed that the Bible teaches that faith alone leads to salvation, beginning with Martin Luther, who in 1517 challenged the Church when he posted his 95 Theses in Germany. There have been wars throughout history resulting in tens of thousands of deaths between Christian sects. The same division about the route to salvation remains today.

Muhammadism

Islam is the third Abrahamic religion, founded by Muhammad after his revelation in the year 610 while meditating on Mount Hira (in modern Saudi Arabia). He stated that the angel Jibril (Gabriel) came to him and commanded that he recite the passage he showed him, although Muhammed had not learned to read. The Qur'an gradually was revealed to him over the next 23 years.

The essential teaching of Muhammad is that there only is one God, Allah, who will judge people after their deaths to determine if they will be allowed into paradise. At first he had no converts, but slowly found people willing to listen as he wandered the city of Medinah. Islam eventually became the world's second largest religion. It has become divided into two sects: Shia and Sunni.

Some believe that Islam is a violent religion, but just like all major religions, its adherents choose between a belief that their faith teaches peace or that it justifies hatred. The vast majority of Muslims are peaceful. One teaching from the Qur'an (5.13) is similar to that of Jesus about turning the other cheek:

We shall always find treachery in others, so pardon them and turn away: surely Allah loves those who are good to others.

We have peered into the essential beliefs of some major religions and their followers. There are a number of themes that appear in all religions, such as leading a righteous life and belief in a force beyond us. But there are other ways that we seek happiness. As we will discuss, there are similarities behind all attempts to find fulfillment. Below is a brief exploration of other paths that will shed some light on the commonality behind them.

Other Paths to Fulfillment

As in religion, there are a number of areas that our personal quests have in common. Beyond what we need to do for survival, many endeavors, whether we label them spiritual or not, have the same purpose: to bring us a sense of inner peace. But no matter how secure we may find ourselves for a brief period of time, our minds soon focus once again on what is missing. We believe that if we only acquire the right possession, engage the right person, or gain the right understanding, or the world changes to meet our expectations, our lives will at last be fulfilled. But regardless of temporary success, we soon return to hoping that our next encounter will result at last in long-term happiness.

Interpersonal Relationships

Our hope in relationships is to engage a missing part of ourselves that we see in others to allow us to become complete – to experience fulfillment by adding what seems lacking, beauty or intelligence, for example. We also may engage in relationships with people we find similar to ourselves to confirm what we see as the best in us. Relationships are threatened – or end – when they no longer fulfill our expectations. We then hope to improve them or we seek others who meet our expectations instead.

Career Advancement

We want to be known as competent individuals who can contribute to the world. Recognition enhances our esteem in the eyes of our community and ourselves. Developing and using our skills is a part of gaining a sense of purpose in life. But our careers enter a rut when they fail to meet our hopes for fulfillment. We then find ourselves stuck or move from one position to another hoping to become useful and appreciated.

Financial Pursuits

Money and its pursuit occupies the thoughts of many of us much of the time. It represents security and an ability to acquire the things we want in life, but when it becomes an end in itself we never can get enough. It can be an obsession to the eclipse of everything else.

Competition

Social order within groups is found in animals as well as among humans. Some people are more natural leaders than others and some more capable. Nearly all of us enjoy competition, and some rise to the top by talent or hard work. If we can't be among the leaders, we align ourselves with contending individuals or teams to experience their victories and defeats. But at best, competition brings only temporary satisfaction.

Involvement in Civic or Political Organizations

Civic and political pursuits allow us to become involved in a purpose larger than ourselves. As we become part of a cause to help our community or country we hope to make the world a better place for us and ours to live. But frustration sets in when we see how little actual effect our efforts have on the real state of the world.

Attempts at Self-Improvement

Throughout our lives we set goals for ourselves and expect that meeting them will bring satisfaction. They can be in areas such as acquiring specific skills, improving our appearance, weight loss or gain, adding strength, or better control of our impulses. Despite our best efforts, it seems that we always fall short of where we want to be. Even when we succeed at one goal, another pops up in our minds, giving us little rest or time to savor our accomplishment.

The Arts

The arts evoke a world that is not easily accessed by words. Music, drama and visual arts have the potential to ignite a place within that goes beyond our concepts and reestablishes a connection to the ongoing flow of reality. Dance enhances our bodily attunement to the rhythm of the universe. The best art shows us that there is a different way of seeing than our customary view. Yet our artistic interests often leave us seeking rather than fulfilled.

Food and Drink

Most of us derive satisfaction from food and drink, which fills the emotional center of our stomach. This was the first place we received nurturance as a child. Our taste and preferences evolved as we matured, based on experience and culture. Food and drink still provide a sense of pleasure and security. Like all areas in which we seek fulfillment, once we are satiated there is little to be derived from consuming more. Nevertheless, our yearning often pushes us beyond satiation.

Personality Cults

There are many leaders we look up to, such as politicians, military heroes, sports personalities, musicians, or scientists. It is easy to put those we admire on a pedestal in our minds, rather than viewing them as human beings with merits and faults. When we fail to have a balanced view of those we admire, we ignore their actions that may be harmful to others, or even to ourselves. This can lead to becoming blind members of a cult.

Body Worship

We often see perfection in the body of a public personality – or even someone we know – and wish that our appearance was more like persons we covet or worship from afar. But those we regard in this way know that they have the same issues with self-esteem as everyone else. Some become self-destructive as they realize that their inner struggles never go away.

Meditation

In meditation we focus on our inner world to release anxiety. This hopefully helps us move to a calmer state. But all types of meditation achieve their intended purpose only temporarily. Our thoughts soon once again turn to anxiety and cause us to look to another time or place as a source of satisfaction. Meditation practice does at times provide a period of peace of mind before we return to the world of thought and anticipation.

Exercise

The long-term effects of a well-regulated exercise routine contribute to an ability to more easily confront our physical challenges. Exercise – when done intensely – has been shown to improve the flow of endorphins in the brain which provide a sense of well-being. But that state of mind only is temporary as it disappears between sessions and – much like a drug – creates a need for itself to be repeated.

Sex

Sex needs no introduction. At best it leads to an "oceanic feeling" with another – or even with the universe – that makes it an obsession for many. But as in all the areas we have discussed, sex is not always the maximum experience we want it to be. It can become routine as its glow fades.

Massage

The sensations of our mind not only are a part of our brain but are experienced through-out the body. Tension and relaxation are physical as well as mental. Massage temporarily allows the body – or parts of it – to relax. But soon our self-imposed tension returns.

Yoga

Yoga means "yoke" in Sanskrit. The practice of yoga is about bridging the divide between our mental and physical selves. There are many types of yoga. Some include physical exertion, stretching, or breathing. Many teachers consider er meditation a type of yoga. Like all efforts at self-improvement, yoga exercises feel good for a while but our mind soon focuses once again on what is lacking in our lives.

Therapies

The dictionary tells us that therapy is "treatment intended to relieve or heal a disorder." The "disorder" treated may be mental, physical or both. As noted for all the other areas discussed, therapies can help us for a while before we return again to seeing our glass half empty rather than half full.

Consciousness-altering Drugs

These drugs are intended to provide an alternative reality to the way we normally perceive the world. Sometimes they allow us to relax, and sometimes they provide a sense of heightened awareness that makes us more tense. An alternative perspective can be beneficial because it expands our view and understanding of the world, but many people are uncomfortable having their view expanded.

Seeking Truth

We each have a philosophy, although we don't usually call it by that name. Our philosophy could be, for example, that people we place in a certain category are good or bad, or that our actions do or do not have an effect on the world. We engage with other people, the media, books, and other sources to get a sense of what really is true, both for information and to improve our lives based on greater understanding. But truth-seeking is a never ending process. Just as we believe we gain insight, the world challenges the truths we thought we had found. One possibility is to open ourselves to changing our views as we gain more information, while another is staying with our preconceptions and clinging to the truths we hold, regardless of the evidence around us.

What All Paths Have in Common

The purpose of all paths is to bring us to a more perfect place. Our assumption is that we are imperfect human beings; that we need to change ourselves or our world to bring us happiness; that we fall short, or in the view of many religions, we are "sinners." We hope for our paths to move us from the ordinary to the extraordinary.

Our paths include a goal we hold in our mind and a route that we tread in its pursuit. Behind all goals is a hope for the experience of fulfillment. Religious pilgrims have made tortuous journeys to Jerusalem, to Santiago de Compostela, to Mecca, and other spots that are considered holy to attain inner peace. In our worldly pursuits we likewise aspire to a sense of personal fulfillment.

Hinduism teaches that we rotate through incarnations until we at last arrive last at an ultimate sense of peace, while Buddhism promotes inner peace through meditation. The Egyptians believed in a perfect afterlife surrounded by servants and the artifacts of life on earth. The Greeks held that how we act while on earth results in our souls descending into eternal torture or reward in the underworld. Canaanite and Hebrew worshipers believed they could extirpate their sins and find salvation by sacrificing animals or other items of value to the gods. The Christians substituted Jesus for this sacrifice, while they and Muslims hold that fulfilling the will of God admits followers to heaven.

Non-religious paths have similar goals of inner peace and fulfillment. Many people do not consider themselves complete without meaningful relationships. We seek fulfilling work and may find ourselves unhappy when forced to perform rote tasks for a living. We often see money as a panacea and think that accumulating enough will bring internal – as well as external – security. We believe that if we – or those individuals or teams with which we identify – succeed at competition we will experience happiness. When we equate our own interests with the success of our communities, states, or nations, we see their success as our own. We think that improving ourselves enough will secure happiness. We rely on the arts to bring us a sense of fulfillment beyond the mundane. Food and drink give us a temporary sensation of pleasure. We worship those who seem to exude confidence and gain confidence through them for a while. As did the Greeks, we experience beauty in what we think of as a perfect body, but to the dishonor of our own. Meditation temporarily brings us to a truth that cannot be expressed by words. Exercise provides relief from stress for a while. Sex can bring short-term release though we continually pursue it. Massage allows us a temporary reprieve from tension. Yoga provides a vision of relaxation that disappears when we re-enter our daily lives. Numerous therapies provide an alternative perspective on our situation for a limited time. Consciousness-altering drugs have the potential to provide greater insight than our usual view. We seek the truth in hope that it will bring us a greater sense of certainty.

But despite our lifelong attempts, none of our paths ever really brings us long-term fulfillment.

Regardless of temporary satisfaction, our minds soon return to discontent – to emphasizing what is lacking in our lives. We thus participate in a continuous cycle of aspiration and failure, lifting ourselves up and being let down while hoping to lift ourselves up once again.

Every religion – and our every longing – hints at what we seek in the deepest registers of our minds: a hope for a lasting state of fulfillment or inner peace. Many of us have resigned ourselves to the possibility that the only real peace we will achieve is our final rest. But no one knows for certain what comes after the body dies. Our ideas about death only express our best understanding of our ultimate destination.

In this life, we use words and concepts to frame our thoughts as we consider if we are happy. Our anxiety still reflects the question we asked as children:

Are we there yet?

And the adult version:

Have we yet reached a point where we are

satisfied with our lives?

There is a vast difference between the idea of fulfillment and its experience. The words we use to describe our progress fail to provide what we really seek.

Thus we are left wondering what satisfaction and fulfillment really are like. Such concepts only skim the surface of the depth of feeling for which we hope. They cannot penetrate to the deepest level of experience. They never can fully capture our most significant aspirations.

All of our paths have their most essential goal in common. We seek inner peace, believing at a place within that there is something missing yet to be accomplished at some other time or place. This is the experience of suffering discussed by Buddhism and of hell described by many religions.

The dichotomy between where we are and where we want to be is an essential element of what it means to be human. The gap between the present and our hope for the future permeates our lives.

The path we choose is based on pursuing an image of what we seek rather than the feeling we really want. As each of our paths fails we then seek another.

Our perpetual yearning has become part of our makeup because it has led to the successful evolution of our species. We are born to be problem solvers. It is better to eat than be eaten, so we have adapted to continually focus on what we must do to survive. We have learned to procure our food supply and create shelters to protect ourselves from the hostile elements of nature. This has led to creation of a civilization that protects us but that we also condemn for creating a bit of hell on earth.

Tilting at Windmills

Most of us are familiar with the story of **Don Quixote**, the hero of the great novel by Miguel Cervantes published in 1605. By the time it was written the legendary knights of the middle ages, who traveled in a quest to right the wrongs of the world, lived on only in the romantic novels of the day.

Don Quixote represents a seeker on the ultimate illusory path. Our hero fills his head with visions of a romantic chivalrous past that he imposes on the world around him. He is guided by his belief in a reality that he creates in his mind as he remains oblivious of all evidence to the contrary.

And so each of us – this writer included – construct the world of our hopes and aspirations. We believe that our paths will lead us to fulfillment. But at the end of each path – if we do arrive there – awaits disillusionment. Our efforts to achieve happiness – at best – may lead to temporary success but most often to disappointment. For those with the fortitude to dust ourselves off and reconfigure our path, we once again ride off in a new direction toward our reward. We continue to pursue our ultimate goal as it remains just out of reach.

The paths we tread – in the best of circumstances – lead to lasting relationships, financial security, or long-term health. But they fail to provide the ultimate inner fulfillment we seek because it is always just one more adventure away. For those fortunate enough to achieve our major goals, our minds will focus on the next, and then once again on the next, postponing our ultimate satisfaction until some vague time in the future.

Thus we engage in a continuous cycle of the birth, death, and rebirth of our deepest ambition throughout this lifetime and – if some religions are correct – into the next. We may tell ourselves we've achieved great victories, but the windmills of our minds challenge us to charge yet once again. They remain unvanquished as we wonder why our goal of spiritual fulfillment eludes us.

And then we once again tell ourselves that if we just have that one more experience, or reach that one more goal, fulfillment will be ours.

What keeps us from what we really want in this moment is our assumption that it only can occur in the future or be provided by a source outside of ourselves. But, rather, we can at any time reach within and evoke that experience.

Thus we already are where we want to be, except in our minds. If we so choose we can acknowledge our essential spiritual nature to provide the certainty we seek in this moment. But that would take a willingness simply say that here and now are enough. Because we fail to do this there is no arriving – only the journey.

And so our journey continues.

We play the game 'Existence' to the end – of the beginning.
— John Lennon, from TOMORROW NEVER KNOWS, BASED ON

THE TIBETAN BOOK OF THE DEAD

THE GOAL

Behind all of our paths is the same goal.

There are many terms we use to describe what we seek: happiness, success, peace, truth, freedom, connectedness, satisfaction, fulfillment, salvation, spiritual awakening, an experience of God – the list is endless. Each term has a different meaning in our thoughts but they all point to the same place within. We use words to describe our ultimate objective, but it is not words or ideas we really want; it is the feeling behind them.

We start life feeling fully connected to our surroundings. Then we develop a sense of separateness and create an identity – or self – that we try to perpetuate and protect. We begin to experience the world more by concept than direct interaction. We then set ourselves on a path to return to that sense of fulfillment we believe we once knew.

As we mature we focus on the skills needed to navigate an uncertain world. But we also long to renew our original view in the hope that it might bring inner peace. We pursue numerous avenues to that end – some spiritual and some wholly of this world. When one fails to yield results we turn to another, but all paths ultimately fail to take us where we really want to go.

Everything we think we know is based on concepts we hold in our minds, whether about ourselves, others, the world, the purpose for which we live, or our relationship with a force beyond us. Because reality is infinite, our concepts never can encompass it. They cannot accurately reflect what is in the minds of people or describe objective reality if such a thing exists, but they can become more accurate as a result of thoughtful communication with others and careful observation. Even the brightest among us acknowledge that there is a limit to what we know. As Stephen Hawking stated during a 2006 lecture at the Institute for Advanced Study that displayed his humor and humanity:

To ask what happened before the beginning of the universe would become a meaningless question.

Since our concepts are limited to the confines of our minds, there is more that we don't know than we do know. These limits include the realm of science and mathematics. Our concepts are based in the past, as are our understanding of the universe and the force that governs it. This is why they always fall short. To move closer to the truth we must be willing to acknowledge their limits, including those about our world, ourselves, our thoughts, and our emotions.

Since none of our concepts lead to fulfill-ment, that only can happen in a place beyond them. Knowing this, we can begin to consider the possibility of directly identifying and evok-ing our ultimate goal. When we truly understand what we seek, we can begin to focus on bringing that into our actions rather than expecting our actions to bring it to us.

"Easy to say," you might protest, "But how do I get there from here? How can I achieve something that cannot easily be described?"

We previously discussed what in psychology and mythology is called "the eternal return," where the hero comes home from a journey having learned significant lessons after a series of life changing adventures. Ulysses returns to his native island of Ithaca a wiser man after his tortuous voyage. Dorothy arrives back at her farm in Kansas having learned: "There is no place like home!"

A return to what we consider our lost state of happiness is behind our hopes, searches and aspirations. It is held as an expectation deep in our minds as we compare it with our daily experience. And because we really can't go home again we perpetually are disappointed, except for brief periods of great adventure, great achievement, great love, great interaction, or great insight. These events don't bring fulfillment themselves, but at these times we allow it to well up within us. Soon we return to our chronic state of anticipation, hoping for a satisfaction we always believe exists at some time or place other than the here and now. We continually try to kick the ball as we move it just beyond our own reach.

At rare times happiness seems to come on its own. We feel connected to our world and selves as our minds provide a glimpse of what we seek. At these moments we appreciate our life and world as we experience fulfillment.

Idol worship is not only a practice from the past, but is present in each of us. Our idols evoke the happiness and certainty we seek. Whether they be religious leaders, teachers, celebrities, or political figures, we place them on a pedestal above us. They represent God on earth, the perfect parent, an answer to the world's problems, the self-confidence we lack, or the ideal human form. We experience fulfillment while in their company or when we hold them in our thoughts. We fear that our lives will lose meaning with their demise. But they all know that they also – at least at times – are plagued by the same self-doubt as everyone else.

We allow ourselves happiness when we believe that our expectations are met, and plunge into unhappiness when we believe they fall short. Our experience of fulfillment has much to do with the view we adopt.

Thus we divide our world in a number of ways to help us simplify and comprehend it. But when we pay close attention to the reality before us, we may find that these divisions actually do not exist. Then we can ask ourselves whether we would rather maintain our view of the world as one that is divided, which has a negative effect on us and others, or adopt a more wholistic view based on the reality before us that has the potential to bring us closer to the fulfillment we seek.

Some Areas into Which We Divide the World

GOOD AND EVIL

Our cultures and traditions – religious and

non-religious – provide examples of good and evil and how to overcome malevolent forces. They encourage us to divide people we should trust from those we should distrust. Our morality tales warn of the devil within whom we bring to life as we succumb to evil. Abraham, Moses, Jesus, Muhammed, Socrates, Confucius, and Buddha, plus all our modern heroes, show us how to follow the righteous path. But in the real world good and evil are not so clear. When we look at others – and ourselves – with less judgment and more openness we come closer to seeing people as they really are. We find they do not fit neatly into our categories. Their complexity makes our judgments less certain. As we bring more compassion to others – all of whom have human failings like us – we experience compassion for ourselves. We see people as more fully human, and realize that the categories into which we divide them are based more on our desire for simplicity than their true nature. A phrase that expresses this principle is attributed to the Buddha:

Have compassion for all human beings, rich and poor alike; all have their suffering.

61

THE SPIRITUAL AND THE MUNDANE

Life takes on greater meaning when our actions are motivated by a larger purpose. It is common to believe that some people and places are spiritual while the rest are ordinary. We can become so focused on a rigid view that our vision narrows and we miss much of reality. Both those of us who are religious and non-religious judge others as we hope that they see the good in us. Our view of the world often corresponds more to our judgments than what is in front of us, and as we divide it we create discomfort in our own minds. Real spirituality acknowledges the presence of the divine in all people and places. It inspires us to find good even in those we consider wicked or beneath us. As we acknowledge the good in others and the world we experience the good within us. Genesis 1:31 tells us:

Then God looked over all he had made, and saw that it was very good.

THOUGHT AND EMOTION

We usually consider thoughts and emotions to be opposites. But our emotions correspond to how we think about the world. When we view people and situations positively we feel optimistic, but when our view is negative we cast a dim light within. Spirituality is not about putting ourselves above life's struggles but about bringing a sense of connection and appreciation to our encounters. If we see life as "brutal and short," to quote Thomas Hobbs from his *Leviathan*, negativity will affect our thoughts and actions. But when we bring less judgment to what we do and feel – even to our anxiety – a sense of calm begins to pervade our minds. Our everyday life – with its ups and downs, its excitements and disappointments, its rewards and risks – rarely is calm. As we recognize the validity of our emotions, and thus of ourselves, we bring an undercurrent sense of peace to all we do.

LIFE AND DEATH

We were part of the earth before our appearance as individuals and again will become part of it when we leave. But even for our brief sojourn on this planet we never stop being part of the earth. We breathe the atmosphere around us in and out as we take in nutrients and expel waste. Our true nature is ongoing change before, during and after what we think of as our separate lives. Over countless millennia life forms have evolved more successful means of self-preservation. Human awareness is part of that success. We are the species that looks back at our history, anticipates our future, and plans for our demise. What we call consciousness is an ever-present aspect of who we are. But lest we become too arrogant, we need to remind ourselves that our essential physical nature is dust. In a very real way there is no death, but only a continual change of form. As stated in GENESIS 3:19:

By the sweat of your face you shall eat bread, till you return to the ground, for out of it you were taken; for you are dust and to dust you shall return.

THE GOAL

HEAVEN AND HELL

Many religions promise heaven as a reward for resisting temptation. Some wait for the Messiah to bring peace to the earth. But we create our own hell by judging and thus separating ourselves from people and the world. We also experience hell as we judge ourselves. Whether or not there is a heaven and hell somewhere other than on this earth, we continually fluctuate between experiencing both. If there is a heaven, we will bring our habit of judgment with us when we arrive, so our essential experience will remain the same. We can begin to move past our mental pain as we engage in appreciation of this world we have been given that nurtures and sustains us. The Qur'an, Surah 16:10, tells us:

It is He who sends down rain from the sky. From it you drink, and out if it (grows) the vegetation on which you feed your cattle. With it He produces for you corn, olives, date-palms, grapes and every kind of fruit.

FORGIVENESS AND BLAME

Some people who consider themselves religious – and many others – use their beliefs to condemn others and their actions. In their righteousness they think they are entitled to decide who is good and bad and perhaps even who deserves to live or die. But as we condemn others we experience the condemnation we create. Every human being errs. Those who err chronically in a way that harms, or has the potential to harm others, need to be separated from society until they demonstrate they can be trusted. Our failure to forgive may or may not affect others but it definitely hurts us and leaves us stuck in the past. As we see this we can begin to move into a mode of forgiveness that cleanses us. But forgiveness as an experience is different from the concept. Asking ourselves what forgiveness really feels like at the deepest level may reveal a place within that provides what we seek. We allow our hearts to open – and let ourselves breathe deeply – as we remember that blame hurts us most of all. The Christian Bible, in Matthew 7:1-3, states:

Judge not, that you be not judged.

LOVE AND HATE

We seek love from others, especially those we see as bringing out the best in us and those who meet our standards for what we want in a partner or friend. But our love often turns to hate as our partner or friend reveals traits previously not seen. The main result of our hate is harm to ourselves. As more qualities of others are revealed, more of us also is revealed. We then choose whether or not to accept an expanding idea of who they and we are. When we hold everyone to high standards it may become hard to find anyone worthy of our love, and when we deny the loving part of ourselves we deprive life to an essential element within. As our ability to love expands we open to a deeper experience of ourselves. Parmahansa Yogananda tells us:

Affirm divine calmness and peace. Send out only thoughts of love and goodwill if you want to live in peace and harmony.

US AND THEM

We divide people into those we think are like us and those we think are not. But as we acknowledge our commonality with all people we expand our idea of our tribe to include more of humanity. We can choose to further only our own interests and of those who seem like us, or take the larger view that the needs of all human beings also are our needs. We can advance our own interests only temporarily until we run up against the reality that the interests of all are intertwined. In each moment we choose to maintain a façade of separateness or acknowledge our common humanity. And in a very real way – seen from our original viewpoint – we are the other person. As we peer into the soul of another ours becomes more transparent.

FREEDOM AND CONSTRAINT

Regardless of whether we are physically free, we only become truly free when we escape from the entrapment of our minds. The experience of freedom cannot be captured by words, only pointed at. Many people who have been imprisoned — the Apostle Paul, Boethius, Gandhi, Martin Luther King, Nelson Mandela, Viktor Frankl — have written about how their minds remained free. When we focus on our limitations or our past we become entrapped in a prison of our own making, but when we identify with our deeper essence we become free. Words only can hint at our true nature because who we really are is all of creation itself. When aware of this it becomes reflected in our view and expressed in our actions. According to Viktor Frankl, in his book *Man's Search for Meaning:*

Everything can be taken from a man but one thing: the last of the human freedoms — to choose one's attitude in any given set of circumstances, to choose one's own way.

WISDOM AND IGNORANCE

We look to others for wisdom about the world and how to conduct our lives. But when what others tell us rings most true is when it corresponds with our own inner sense of what is right. All we really know of the world is what we hold in our thoughts, but if we were to summarize what our best teachers have tried to convey it might be faith in our inner wisdom – in our ability to find and pursue our own paths. On our journey the dignity of all human beings is our true moral compass.

CHILD AND ADULT

Young children allow themselves to experience each emotion fully and then move on to the next. Although we generalize about children they all are different and act differently. Most respond to their creative impulse more fully than adults. The way they talk, act and move shows that they are not yet set in their sense of self. They remind us of a part of ourselves that we largely have abandoned. This is why most adults enjoy and learn from their company. In Matthew 18:3, Jesus admonishes his followers to learn from children:

Unless you change and become like little children, you never will enter the kingdom of heaven.

THE GOAL

REWARD AND PUNISHMENT

We want to punish others to confirm our own righteousness. But in making others suffer we only temporarily distance ourselves from our own suffering. When we allow ourselves to experience our connection to others we move toward healing as we share their pain and pleasure. When we seek to lift others and recognize the best in them we also confirm what is best in us.

BELIEF AND FAITH

Our beliefs are our ideas about the world – and a possible place beyond it – and how to navigate them. When we cling to our beliefs we obstruct our view of reality as we impose ideas from our past on a constantly changing world. Our beliefs make our actions less accurate and effective. Faith, on the other hand, is a willingness to encounter others and the world as we find them. Faith affirms our ability to move beyond preconceptions. Faith conquers all obstacles on our path as we reaffirm our vision of interconnectedness that is our most essential view.

MALE AND FEMALE

When young we learn – either by lesson or example – the proper way for boys and girls to act. Most of us are taught the link between males and aggression or females and sensitivity. We learn to deny the part of ourselves that doesn't fit with what we believe is our identity. But there are no "male" or "female" emotions – just human emotions. Recently we have begun to respect gender identities never previously considered. Although homosexuality has been known for the duration of civilization, bisexuality, transsexuality, pansexuality, and kinky sexuality, among others, are newer terms that emerged as we peeled back deeper aspects of human identity. There are no doubt more gender roles yet to be identified. But our gender is not the essence of who we are. That is found in a place beyond our identity. Our real self encompasses multiple aspects of who we are. If we choose, we can evoke the compassion within us toward all aspects of others – and ourselves – as we acknowledge that we are more than our identity.

THE RACIAL DIVIDE

We divide ourselves into races so we can know who is like us and who is not. Race also can be an excuse to discriminate against others and treat them as less than fully human. Other types of discrimination include religion, country of origin, economic disparities, disabilities, lifestyles, and political affiliations. When we seek someone to blame for our discomfort we always will be able to find a victim. But discriminating against others doesn't help our situation – it only temporarily distances us from our own suffering. When we focus on people as individuals without judgement we see them more clearly and feel better about ourselves. When we become aware of the danger of the divisions we have created, we can move toward a world where we improve the lives of all in areas such as education, the economy, health and the environment. We find that we have more in common than we have differences as we move past the resentment that causes us all great harm. Those we consider to be within the same groups also have many difficulties among themselves. In Africa, genocide due to numerous civil wars in places such as Ethiopia, Rwanda, and Sudan has resulted in the slaughter of millions. Persecution within China by emperors and communist leaders has led to countless deaths. Natives of both North and South America slaughtered other tribes. And of course there have been endless atrocities by members of what we consider the white "race" against each other. To understand human conflict, we must peer more deeply into the personalities of people. Then we see that by nature we harbor resentments that we project onto whichever scapegoats are most convenient. But respecting others leads to a world in which we all are respected, including ourselves. Seeing all people as fellow human beings leads to a world of greater peace and progress for everyone. As we embrace diversity we embrace multiple aspects of ourselves. As stated eloquently by Martin Luther King Jr.:

Darkness cannot drive out darkness; only light can do that. Hate cannot drive out hate; only love can do that.

TRUTH AND FALSEHOOD

It is hard for our minds to conceive of nothing; they have evolved to create models of the world that we use to guide us. We do our best to understand and describe truth and this has led to much of our success. Those who use truth to their advantage have been able to understand their environment and rely on the past to predict the future; this has made them more likely to survive. The best information we glean from our experience and that of others is called science. But if our actions are mainly reactions to others then they, and not we, govern our lives. Our understanding must be based on what we see – balanced with what we are told – if we are to continue to succeed. Even so, there always will be much we don't know. Our world is constantly changing. When we approach it without preconditions we are rewarded with greater attunement to reality. Approaching others with appreciation for their inner wisdom provides additional guidance.

TEACHER AND STUDENT

From our youth we strive to learn how to identify and move toward meaningful goals. The role of our teachers is to guide us in attaining the knowledge and skills to advance in that direction. But teaching that dwells on rote impedes our progress toward greater insight and achievement. In spiritual matters we seek to reignite that place within that reconnects us with the understanding we carry from birth. Our best teachers and teachings inspire confident exploration and self-discovery rather than telling us what to think or believe about our values and life direction.

SUCCESS AND FAILURE

While we live, nothing and no one can defeat us unless we decide we are defeated. No matter how low we may have been driven – by others or ourselves – we can at some point begin once again to identify and move toward our goals. But first we must clarify a sense of purpose to guide our actions. Otherwise our accomplishments will leave us unfulfilled. Success never is possible unless we plan our steps. There will be real or imagined setbacks to which we can best respond if we have our goal firmly in mind. Every achievement leads to the start of another. Returning to our state of connection to others and the world is our ultimate guide.

FORM AND SUBSTANCE

We carry an ideal in our minds of how we want our lives to look and feel. We pursue perfection, but perfection can be a friend or enemy. We seek perfection in nearly everything we hope to encounter – a perfect romance, a perfect friend, a perfect job, a perfect meal, perfect music, a perfect work of art, a perfect setting in nature, or a perfect model of ourselves. But there is no perfection in the real world; from nature's viewpoint all is as it needs to be. By opening to a reality beyond our compulsion for perfection we experience people and objects for their intrinsic worth, which is what we most want for ourselves. Some traditions teach that spirituality takes a specific form, or perhaps one that is benign, but we were born to live fully in each new moment. According to Neemkaroli Baba:

The best form in which to worship God is every form.

PAST, PRESENT AND FUTURE

We divide our ideas of the world into the past, present and future, but in reality there only is a continuous series of events that passes through the present. More accurately, there is one ongoing event that originated at the beginning of time. Past and future only can be experienced in the present. It is by our thoughts we create our world and our idea of ourselves. The objective world — if it exists — remains forever unknown, although by paying close attention and listening to the well-considered views of others we may bring our concepts closer to reality. This moment — the only moment we know — has no name, just as God has no name in some religions. Yet we live primarily in the world of labels and thoughts. We must go through our reactions and emotions – what we call joy, happiness, sadness, and grief – because that is how we are designed. But allowing what we experience – rather than labeling and blocking it – permits us to be fully human and then move on. In a letter to a friend one month before he died in 1955, Albert Einstein wrote:

For people like us who believe in physics, the separation between past, present and future has only the importance of an admittedly tenacious illusion.

OUR MANY SELVES

One of the most famous sentences ever written was by René Descartes in his ***Discourses:*** "I think therefore I am." But his "I" was no proof of the existence of a separate self – it was just another assumption. It is this assumption of the separate self that impedes our spiritual understanding. All we know about who we are – and of the source of all life – are our thoughts about them.

There are many selves within us that sometimes function in harmony but also often strive against each other. These selves are aspects of our minds and not actual physical divisions. They have been given numerous names by different traditions. The real Self is not a separate being; it is our true nature that transcends all aspects of who we are.

What we consider our separate physical self interacts – and reacts – with our surroundings, much like a spontaneous child and just like every plant and animal. This roughly corresponds to the id of Freud. The self-conscious part of us – the ego of Freud – is the one we create in our minds as a separate being with a past, present and future. This corresponds to the Son in the Christian trilogy. The self of conscience – the superego of Freud, or the God Father in Judaism, Christianity and Muhammadism – tells us how to act, and judges us when we fall short.

The Higher Self looks over the others. This Self corresponds to the Holy Spirit in Christianity, the Shekinah in Judaism, the Transcendental Self of Hinduism and the Great Mother described by

THE GOAL

Jungian psychology. This is the all-forgiving entity in many cultures and religions, also personified by Mary in Christianity. This Self always is present and witnesses us and our world. She is the light that pervades all darkness. It is She who forgives our transgressions without question. From the view of the Higher Self nothing needs to be hidden or different, but as we allow her to infuse our reality all is transformed – the ordinary becomes seen as divine. This Self is consciousness looking back at itself. It is present at those times when we are willing to recognize it and at times when we are not. The avatars of the great world religions understood that this Self is the most essential part of our nature. This is the all-encompassing One God who is the essence of the universe and is the object of self-realization in Eastern religion. It is to this Self we are born and intuitively long to return. This is the God referred to in 1 John 4:16 of the Christian Bible that tells us:

God is Love.

The Nature of Forgiveness

Our Higher Self already forgives us but it is our decision at all times whether or not to let this forgiveness in. Contrary to what we might think, forgiveness does not give us license to commit foul acts. Instead, it changes our view and actions to be more respectful for all that exists. Even if forgiveness comes from without – or from a God above us – it is not felt unless we accept it. Forgiveness is a place of full feeling – of our anger, our pain, our sadness, our joy – and allowing all that is in us full recognition. As we acknowledge our faults they are forgiven so we can move on. We can't forgive ourselves in the future – only in this moment. According to Gandhi:

The weak never can forgive. Forgiveness is an attribute of the strong.

The Nature of Freedom

Those who see themselves as oppressed or downtrodden long for liberation and celebrate it when they become free. But just as the Israelites quickly forgot the freedom they had been given and lapsed into idol worship, most of us forget what is right with our lives — even in the best of circumstances — and emphasize what we see as missing. Freedom is more than just a concept; it is a willingness to appreciate the lives we have been given and to act in harmony with that understanding.

The Nature of Truth

There is one Truth but infinite ways to frame it. We'll never know for certain the entire truth because all is filtered through our perceptions. We adopt a narrow frame while ignoring much of the larger reality around us. There are limits to observations done by the naked eye and even by those of our most advanced scientific instruments. As the scientists behind quantum mechanics have asserted, the process of observation itself alters our view. But when aware of that we can open to the possibility of a larger Truth beyond our perceptions. According to Werner Heisenberg, in **Physics and Philosophy:**

It never will be possible by pure reason to arrive at some absolute truth.

Spirituality and Democracy

Democracy is the political system most compatible with spirituality because it is based on the principle of total respect for every human being. Democracy is rooted in the Greek term "Government by the People." In the words of Lincoln, in his Gettysburg Address, if we maintain democracy then:

Government of the people, by the people, for the people, shall not perish from the earth.

Democracy's survival depends on each of us acting respectfully toward others, often in the face of different world views and others not being respectful toward us. We can resolve our differences only when we listen to each other and begin to focus on our common needs. Economic concerns often result in people looking after their own interests and ignoring the need to work together to guarantee equal opportunity for all. In our day there are a number of countries once considered democratic that have regressed because of a lack of a shared vision that addresses the needs of everyone. Beyond that, democracy affords us an opportunity to interact with others as equals. This brings recognition to our essential self – the being beneath our views and identity – which is who we really are. Hopefully a resurgence of commitment to democratic principles in other nations will be inspired by the longest lasting democratic nation, the United States.

Spirituality and Anger

When the world doesn't meet my expectations, anger sometimes comes up in me. No matter how hard we try or how well we plan, things still will go wrong. I may find that I need to express my concern in strong terms - or even fight - when confronted with a danger to myself or others. But expressing my anger never decreases it. If I simply allow my anger to well up – without judging it – it soon subsides. I can look back and see that does not make me an "angry" person. I soon am able to return to a sense of balance. There is no such thing as "justified" anger because its main effect is on me. We don't need to carry the anger from another time or person within us. We can accept our feelings – and those of others – and then move on. According to Nelson Mandela:

Resentment is like drinking poison and hoping it will kill your enemies.

Spirituality and Humor

Humor is an essential part of spirituality. It is an ability to distance ourselves from what we see as the seriousness and tragedy of our lives when, as is the case most of the time, they need not be serious or tragic. If we are dependent on others or circumstances for happiness, then our episodes of joy will be brief. I find that I often catch myself – and then laugh at myself – for taking it all too seriously; for setting unreasonably high expectations for others, circumstances and myself. Once I see that, I usually am able to return to a sense of harmony. But at times I seem unable to do that and have to wait until my mind is willing to come back into balance. As often stated in these pages, the only time we can do anything is this moment.

Spirituality and Leadership

There are many spiritual leaders who will tell us they represent the one true path, and their flock often will support that view. They believe they are the white sheep while the black sheep remain on the other side of the fence. All other paths are seen as naïve at best and evil at worst. We cut ourselves off from others and much of creation as we assert that only our way – and thus we – represent the truth. But the spirit that dwells throughout the universe – or the transcendental God who is everywhere – interacts continually with all elements of creation regardless of the divisions we create in our minds. Real spiritual leadership recognizes that. The true God is connected to every human being and every thing. If you think your God directs you to hate others, you are worshipping a false god. Matthew 5:45 states:

He makes his sun to shine on the evil and the good, and sends his rain on the just and unjust.

Spirituality and Death

Perhaps our most frequently pondered question is what happens after the body dies. Despite the multiple answers provided by our traditions, the most honest answer remains that no one really knows. Many people report having "near death" experiences, after which they return, stating that their lives were permanently changed. These incidents include being clinically dead and believing that life was at an end, where one's entire life flashes through the mind. They result from temporarily giving up our attachment to this world, including our idea of who we are, and just floating free of past and future in our minds. Yet these experiences really are not death itself.

But not knowing what happens after death actually has the potential to bring us comfort. It forces us to focus on the world before us, of which, if we are honest, we know nothing except our limited concepts. As we acknowledge our lack of real understanding it evokes uncertainty and humility. We begin to see that all real knowledge about the nature of the universe is beyond us. Then we are forced to function with greater respect for all that surrounds us – including people we consider our friends and enemies. We return to seeing everything and everyone with the great awe with which we began.

Our Choice

In this moment and every moment we have a choice.

We can maintain a belief in our separate identity or open to the possibility that the lives and needs of everyone are interconnected. We can maintain that the force governing the universe exists somewhere outside of us, or that it functions within and through us. We can hold to a view that our ultimate goals - happiness, fulfillment, and inner peace - can be experienced only in the past or future, or acknowledge in this moment that the state we seek already is our essential nature.

We can evoke a distant and judgmental God to guide us, or one who is present and forgiving. When God is at a distance, fulfillment perpetually exists at a place and time other than here and now. When ours is a forgiving God, what we most want already is accomplished.

Our essential vision influences our everyday thoughts and actions. If we believe that we and our needs are separate from others, we will function in isolation, unable to experience the connection we seek. When we see God as somewhere other than where we are, we never can be touched by the compassion we most want. If we believe that fulfillment always is somewhere else, it will continue to be lacking wherever we are.

But if aware of our connection to others and the universe, we will be able to bring that view to the pursuit of our most significant goals. If we comprehend that the force which governs everything includes us, it will support us in the pursuit of our most noble vision. Seeing that we can fulfill our ultimate purpose in this moment frees us from the fetters of the past and our perpetual concern for the future.

THE GOAL

We choose the view that fulfillment always awaits us at some other time and place, or that it is ever-present. To the extent we open to an expanded idea of ourselves and affirm our connection to the universe - experientially not intellectually - we clarify and live our purpose. We see that what we most want - unity with others and all that exists - already is accomplished. Our pain, sorrow and loneliness yield to the connectedness of this moment, then this moment, and then the next.

The traumas of our past have no hold over our minds unless we so choose. We cannot change anything that we or anyone has done or felt, but we can bring compassion and allow ourselves a full experience of our feelings in the present. This enhances our lives as we no longer await permission to fully live. It restores our humanity as we return to our most essential Self.

All paths - all truths - that we are taught are someone's idea of spirituality. As we put those aside we begin to clarify our own truth, which may not easily be put into words. We may find that the state we seek is nameless but still the most essential element of who we are. If we're connected to everything we're also connected to the force - or Being - that put us here.

No one is immune to the pitfalls into which we all stumble due to limited vision, including this writer. But our ultimate goal remains a return to the undifferentiated consciousness with which we began. There is no gap between where we are and where we most want to be except in our minds. This is not a "mystical" view, but one of the real world based on direct interaction that serves as a guide for how best to conduct our lives. It is a return to the world we knew before we labeled it - to our most basic nature.

This is the most significant insight of the founders of our religions, but is an essential part of everyone. Religion can be a means by which we give over responsibility for our views and actions to another person or belief system, or it can be a vehicle for each of us to explore and confirm our most basic truths.

The bodies in which we dwell always will experience the fears and anxieties that flesh is heir to, but that is not our truest nature. Rather, we are the One who never perishes. This understanding is based not on faith, but on direct experience when we pull back our facade of separation. It is what we see when we return to the universal consciousness with which we were born.

When we simply observe, we penetrate the essence of reality - that place beyond words - as we discover a truth that leaves the world of words behind. Perhaps it best can be described as that which is.

Where I Come From

When I was very small and still preverbal I noticed that people were able to influence others at a distance. Although I lacked understanding of the words they used, I wondered how one person could become tense or uncomfortable and convey that mood to another person across the room. I also wondered how people could become unhappy when there was nothing in sight that caused it. What eventually occurred to me was that we experience unhappiness when we hold a negative vision in our minds although nothing negative may be happening in front of us. We carry images around that easily are evoked. Rather than living in the world before us, we live largely in the world of our minds that we impose on reality.

The purpose of language is to share experience. The ability to communicate has enabled the human race to advance far beyond its origins to inhabit most of the earth and create our civilizations. But evolution is not done with us. Language can help us continue on our path of progress, or become the tool that we use to destroy ourselves. We can use it to work together toward a common vision or against each other. It is the means that has allowed us to build the environments in which we dwell, but when our concepts become rigid they leave us unable to move beyond our views from the past to see the people and world before us.

Watch two people talking. Our conversations often center on what we think is wrong and rarely on an appreciation of the world we have been given or how to improve our situation. Thus we rob ourselves of opportunities to experience fulfillment.

There are times when we do allow ourselves happiness. But we often miss chances to move our lives and worlds in the direction we seek because we focus on what is missing, not what is in front of us or where we want to go.

My intent is not to coerce anyone to think or act differently. That is what we already do to ourselves. Rather, my intent is to encourage us to begin observing our world free of preconceptions to the extent possible. This allows us to be more in tune with the nameless reality that exists everywhere. That simple act allows us to move toward fulfillment – our most basic nature that already is surging through us, although we rarely recognize it. When we move beyond a focus on what is negative we simply experience what is in front of us. But this is so rarely done that it takes a special effort. This simple act of observing – rather than judging – is what is most likely to bring fulfillment as well as the continued success of our species. It also is the view most compatible with action based in reality.

When the Israelites wandered the desert, Moses tried at first to resolve all disputes among his thousands of followers. This didn't work, so he divided the judgeship among a number of men he considered wise enough to handle the task (Exodus 18:17-23). Knowing that people often prefer simple and straightforward rules to guide them he ascended Mount Sinai and brought back the Ten Commandments (Exodus 20:1-17). People have been struggling to keep those command-ments ever since, often without success. But dis-cussing and understanding the principles that underlie our morality would be more likely to allow us to apply them successfully in our lives.

Much has been mentioned in these pages about spirituality. Like most people, I follow the principles by which I hope to live when most aware of them, yet often fall short. My view is perhaps best stated by Thomas Aquinas in his **Summa Theologica** (1.8.2.3):

Just as the soul exists wholly everywhere in the body, so God exists wholly in each and every thing.

Below I describe some basic principles of spirituality as I see them. This is a way of framing how we can maintain spirituality in our lives. I think each of us also can find a place of morality within based on an understanding of our unity with others and all of creation. Clearer vision comes when we move aside what we think we know. When we overthrow the tyranny of our thoughts truth becomes more apparent. Our actions may not appear different, but they become a means of expressing our fulfillment rather than seeking it. To be clear, the following are not commandments. Those already have been given.

Ten Spiritual Principles

1. All religions and ideologies are based on a view of universal truths. As we come closer to identifying and living those truths we approach the nature of the Presence who is everywhere. Truth – and God – are found in the direct apperception of all that surrounds us – in the understanding that precedes and supersedes all words.

2. When we revert to our original view, we return to an awareness of the divine presence in our world, others and ourselves. When in touch with our true selves we no longer seek fulfillment. Rather we bring it into our actions. We only can make that choice in this moment.

3. Nothing is as we think it is. What does exist is the ongoing thrust of time and motion. There only is the continuous flow of the one event of which we are a part. The world of things is a fabric of our minds.

4. Happiness, sadness, and every other human emotion courses through us at its own pace.

Fighting our feelings is futile, but allowing them to be there lets them move through us as we – and they – are transformed.

5. All of creation is sacred. Therefore, we try to respect everything and everyone; we cause harm only as needed for survival.

6. Past, present and future only can be experienced in this moment. Fulfillment cannot be attained in the future because it always is the present. Therefore, we honor this moment and all that is in it.

7. All we know of the world is our concepts. Therefore, we keep in mind that we really know nothing. As individuals we only are aware of our view of what is true. Paying attention to the world around us and communicating with others for the purpose of alignment with truth brings us closer to greater understanding, greater compassion and more effective action.

8. There only is now. Therefore, we already are here and now, including our ideas about the past and future.

9. God – or the force that governs the universe – is immutable and everywhere at once. Therefore we all are in God and deserving of utmost respect.

10. Our true or essential Self always is with us. All paths that attempt to lead us there are futile. In the moment we stop seeking we simply experience being here, which is where we long to be and already are. We have arrived home although we never really left. Soon once again the path will beckon as we play the game of existence, realizing that we are on the path and at our goal at the same time.

In some cultures there is a myth that before birth each child already is aware of the truths of the universe, and that our task is to relearn those lessons in our time on earth. So just before birth an angel holds its finger up to each child's lips to remove these truths from its memory. This is the origin of the small indentation – known as the philtrum – on our upper lip.

THE GOAL

As mentioned, children are closest to the Divine. I'd like to leave you with a quote from the 2011 Bat Mitzvah speech of my daughter Bessie, who often reminds me about the importance of being more open-minded:

If you need comfort, God is there.

If you need help trying to decide what to do with your life, God is there.

Even when we are questioning God, God is there.

ABOUT THE AUTHOR

Steve Zolno has been leading groups in spirituality for over forty years. He has a BA from Shimer College and an MA in Educational Psychology from Sonoma State University. This is his fourth book. He can be reached at *thefutureofdemocracy.net.*

CPSIA information can be obtained
at www.ICGtesting.com
Printed in the USA
FSHW010223260321
79793FS